SISTER

زبان خواهر

Wick Poetry First Book Series

DAVID HASSLER, EDITOR

The Local World by Mira Rosenthal	Maggie Anderson, Judge
Wet by Carolyn Creedon	Edward Hirsch, Judge
The Dead Eat Everything by Michael Mlekoday	Dorianne Laux, Judge
The Spectral Wilderness by Oliver Bendorf	Mark Doty, Judge
Translation by Matthew Minicucci	Jane Hirshfield, Judge
hover over her by Leah Poole Osowski	Adrian Matejka, Judge
Even Years by Christine Gosnay	Angie Estes, Judge
Fugue Figure by Michael McKee Green	Khaled Mattawa, Judge
The Many Names for Mother by Julia Kolchinsky Dasbach	Ellen Bass, Judge
On This Side of the Desert by Alfredo Aguilar	Natalie Diaz, Judge
How Blood Works by Ellene Glenn Moore	Richard Blanco, Judge
Sister Tongue زبان خواهر by Farnaz Fatemi	Tracy K. Smith, Judge

MAGGIE ANDERSON, EDITOR EMERITA

Already the World by Victoria Redel	Gerald Stern, Judge
Likely by Lisa Coffman	Alicia Suskin Ostriker, Judge
Intended Place by Rosemary Willey	Yusef Komunyakaa, Judge
The Apprentice of Fever by Richard Tayson	Marilyn Hacker, Judge
Beyond the Velvet Curtain by Karen Kovacik	Henry Taylor, Judge
The Gospel of Barbecue by Honorée Fanonne Jeffers	Lucille Clifton, Judge
Paper Cathedrals by Morri Creech	Li-Young Lee, Judge
Back Through Interruption by Kate Northrop	Lynn Emanuel, Judge
The Drowned Girl by Eve Alexandra	C. K. Williams, Judge
Rooms and Fields: Dramatic Monologues from the War in Bosnia by Lee Peterson	Jean Valentine, Judge
Trying to Speak by Anele Rubin	Philip Levine, Judge
Intaglio by Ariana-Sophia M. Kartsonis	Eleanor Wilner, Judge
Constituents of Matter by Anna Leahy	Alberto Rios, Judge
Far from Algiers by Djelloul Marbrook	Toi Derricotte, Judge
The Infirmary by Edward Micus	Stephen Dunn, Judge
Visible Heavens by Joanna Solfrian	Naomi Shihab Nye, Judge

Sister Tongue

زبان خواهر

Poems by

Farnaz Fatemi

The Kent State University Press

Kent, Ohio

ISBN 978-1-60635-444-5
Manufactured in the United States of America

The Wick Poetry Series is sponsored by the Stan and Tom Wick Poetry Center and the Department of English at Kent State University.

Cataloging information for this title is available at the Library of Congress.

26 25 24 23 22   5 4 3 2 1

In memory of Jamie I. Gross
and for all my sisters—
in blood, in spirit, in tongues.

CONTENTS

FOREWORD BY TRACY K. SMITH

Farnaz Fatemi has long lived in two languages: English and Farsi. Raised
in suburban southern California, she was the "kid with a name no one
tried to get right." Even all these years later, she is the one whose heart is
quickened by Farsi-accented English. In Farsi she is always just arriving
from faraway, moving "carefully, hoping to make just enough sense." In
Sister Tongue, Fatemi shines gorgeous light on the liminal space between
languages, bearing witness to the joy and longing that accompany every
act of translation.

Perhaps poetry is itself an act of translation. Perhaps all poems emerge
from the realization that the terms in which we routinely live fall short
in times when powerful feelings—like love, need, gratitude, and regret—
threaten to overwhelm us. And so, poems swing, they leap, they wander
far afield, they wash over us like whitewater or blow us back like gale-
force wind. They do all these things so that we might be better known to
ourselves.

In Fatemi's voice, this reacquainting of the self with itself takes many
forms. The poem "Untranslated" celebrates cultural inheritance, the ex-
periential wealth of generations, even as it admits the longing brought
on by distance and estrangement:

All the women
who disappeared into the silence inside me,

I pull from the roar of the past.
I make introductions. By which I mean,

I want the foreigner in me
to meet the foreigner in me.

In one of the seven poems bearing the title "Sister Tongue زبان خواهر" Fa-
temi enacts the rapture of being not simply understood in crossing from
one language to the next, but comprehended and claimed:

I move into the language carefully, hoping to make just enough
sense, and my aunt's eyes light up—as if she were me, sounding
out the words, putting one word on the string of words behind the

previous one, hearing the clack of words coming together as a full strand, a whole meaning.

Later in the same poem, Fatemi even finds ways to capture the desire to escape altogether the confines of the known self. She writes, "Allah-o-Akbar. The voice stops dogs in the street, incites admiration, self-erasure."

One of the ways Fatemi's speaker bridges the distances and differences that sit (or flow) between languages is to move across forms. The suite of poems that give the volume its title embodies the lyric meandering and the emotional accretion that characterize the Japanese *zuihitsu* form. Unlike the book's many compact lyrics, which crystallize images and visceral feelings, or move quickly across a field of sound, the *zuihitsu* offers readers a chance to dwell in the speaker's memory and associative intelligence. A lyric poem hurtles toward revelation. The *zuihitsu* moves step by step at the speed of unrushed thought, which is a lot like the movement through a life. Gently, and then more emphatically, understanding overtakes us. We are someplace, knowing something we couldn't have grasped fully by a more succinct route.

From one language, or mood, or context to the next, we all live between states. I find it fitting, then, that the imagination at the heart of *Sister Tongue* is not fixated on putting down roots. Instead, it seeks to find ease, release, even peace in life's constant going. As the speaker of "Immigrant" puts it, "It's stasis that dizzies."

I Name the Eight Muscles of My Tongue

من هشت ماهیچه زبانم را نامگذاری می‌کنم

I NAME THE EIGHT MUSCLES OF MY TONGUE

agnost

I was slow to understand
the phrase, "I speak for myself."
How to believe what I want to say.
Half of my tongue a late bloomer.
The tongue has eight muscles
which move it, four for shape,
four for direction.

diatom

Before I am five I have the sounds
of two alphabets in my mouth
but after I am five speaking is exertion.
I choose English. My aunt pinching
my cheek sits sullen in the back of my mouth.
My grandmother's loving questions lodge
between my canine and molar, a throb.

saltcells

My mother utters lines she believes
she needs to: words formed in her lungs
at birth. Her life unfurls in sentences,
dictation, as-told-to's.
What does she find in translation?
Into English and Spanish and German
Italian and Czech? So many tongues.
Can she remember herself with just one?

allium

My sister's mouth says more than I do,
exhales vivid holler, calls us all

to hear. I hear her and forget the taste
of my own sorrow, imagine I'm healed,
my suffering surpassed.
It was always this way.
I don't remember how it happened.
My sister's mouth: my answers.

lipid

I might have reminded myself
to ask question after question,
talked over all the voices
who seemed not to listen.
If I had known this as a child
I might have ached less for company.
I wanted to know things so I asked.
Not everyone felt this way.
As cells slough off in the mouth
they leave traces behind
to be sopped up or swallowed.
I don't change. I will always
want to know.

chalk

This muscle tells my secrets,
if they're told, cupping truth
to keep it close, prevent it
from being swallowed. It knows,
though sometimes it doesn't know
it knows, what the limits are to telling.
I want to speak in a room where
someone might always be yelling.
How fast to let things out. Who to
talk to, what danger lies underneath.

brine

The place that remembers things
the mind might not have learned.
Tart shame of thinking too hard
about myself. Metallic swig
of betrayal. Like my girlhood
fears, it lives unnamed.
Still it spills what it knows.

slack

I learn to taste the truth
in secret. Give over to mute bliss.
What is silent dwells on the names
it gives each of its selves,
lets them linger
to get them right.

UNTRANSLATED

In the silence of my girlhood, spoons
clattered in glasses of tea.

The squeak of the front door closing.
I was the child

I'd never have. I listened for clues.
I spoke without saying a thing.

I made sounds to fill
the spaces I could see

around everyone. My teeth and eyes
gleamed, face open, a flower.

As if to say to these people,
Speak. Say things I understand.

Their untranslated words whoosh by,
an autumn gust.

Staticky din of English and Farsi
with afternoon fruit and cookies,

my lips mouthing along with them
to pay attention, as I wrote their stories

in my head, rearranged the letters
into meaning. I heard the squished sounds

of a heartbeat in a stethoscope,
pump and thrum.

In the languages
of women I could have been

I felt both lonely and contained.
We were chador-less,

light skinned. All the women
who disappeared into the silence inside me,

I pull from the roar of the past.
I make introductions. By which I mean,

I want the foreigner in me
to meet the foreigner in me.

RADISH GARDEN

i

My mother's postage stamp of radish and chives
was tucked at the edge of the backyard lawn,

a soft mat we played on like our neighbors in the tract,
eternally sprinkler-damp.

How easily she adopted Easter baskets
—hollow bunnies in pink foil, eggs in plastic grass—

wanted us to feel as American
as our friends. Her radishes breached

the soil's surface, their lip-colored tops
humming to me about something.

I understood she had planted them.
She served those spicy round roots

Persian style, with feta and herbs at dinners.
My father was leaving, but I hadn't yet noticed.

ii

I feel under the canopy
of radish leaves in my garden, caress the dirt,

curved tops breaking forth—my first success.
I bring dozens to my mother. Murmur,

those radishes forty years ago? I know you grew them
for yourself, but I found them.

She planted the Easter Bunny
in the earth of our household and tended her radish patch

in the yard out back. Decades from that house
and that yard, I root my hands

back into the soil of those years.
I ask myself, *who do I want to be?*

BORDERS

I know its shape—
my not-country
faraway home.
I know the space
it takes
the snail head
of Tabriz
at the top,
bulbous
spiral of the rest.
I've known
for decades
without knowing,
the way I didn't know
what countries touch
the tender neck,
the belly or the shell
except Iraq
because my cousins
hoped not to die
on that front.

SISTER TONGUE / زبان خواهر

On the plane to Iran, I inventory what I need. Words, ways to speak them, moments when they matter. These are the things I have promised myself I'll remember.

Eshgh. How the word *love* sounds in my other language. I hear the word, the back of my mouth closing in unison with the speaker's *gh,* heart quickens, ribs relax. With a different passport, my eyes move right to left on the page, my tongue tastes different, curls and loops, then drops back into my palate.

Eshgh. The sound of cooing made-up words I could have said to other children when we were young. An intuition. Back when we understood each other no matter how the words were spelled. I meet a woman on the streets in Tehran who's come from New York for a few days. We share the halftones between English and Farsi. I recognize how she points and swears, she understands how I flip my hair. We've only just met. I know I know her.

This is how it feels to sound out joon. To say eshgh-e-man. To tell you I will kiss you when you're asleep.

زبان خواهر

On my first monthlong trip to Iran as a grown woman, with my mother, grandmother, and twin sister, I do not talk much. My grandmother and mother do the work for us, but in the mornings, before getting so exhausted from paying attention that I space out, I listen, to understand. I remember that listening is work too.

We want to cool off from the swelter of boulevards in Tehran. It's June and the air is thick and we feel our manteaus—our almost fashionable coats—shutting us inside. It's early: I haven't yet learned how to wear one without hiding in it. I had thought the pockets were such a good idea—but the extra layers make my hips sweat nonstop. The space under my bra line is soaked. In a small grocery market we linger at the melons. The store sells ice cream cones—lemon hued and rose flavored. My aunt asks me to order my own. She has seen me listening. I do. I don't know what it sounds like: I'm too busy watching the man's face as I speak to see if I'm understood. I am. I remember the ice cream from 25 years before. I move into the language carefully, hoping to make just enough sense, and my aunt's eyes light up—as if she were me, sounding out the words, putting one word on the string of words behind the previous one, hearing the clack of words coming together as a full strand, a whole meaning. She smiles, then whoops one of her half-inhaled, half-screamed laughs. She looks at me and tastes her ice cream. Yells, "Ahf, Farnaz, kafe mikonim! Do you know what kafe means? Oh, Farnaz, kafe is like, 'We are having a blast.' Aren't we?!" I smile, bewildered.

زبان خواهر

Though I've been hearing Farsi all my life, this still happens: I learn how to use a word in the right place, at the right time, and my head feels saffron bright, pure sunlight.

زبان خواهر

The azan, Allah-o-Akbar. The call to prayer.

Allah's not god to me; he's my grandmother's and my great aunt's god: creature with a name I never say. When I've said God, I've said I'm not sure I believed there was one, though I know Amejoon's Allah was real. I heard her say the word, and I saw her kneel into the carpet in her room and pull a chador up around almost everything and leave her hands with her beads and her small Koran in her lap, whispering words about him—to him, with him.

Allah-o-Akbar. The voice stops dogs in the street, incites admiration, self-erasure.

When I'm in Iran the call to prayer is a call to God, an invocation. I join. My blood moves when I hear the phrase, Allah-o-Akbar, sung like music. It's not music. It's the sound of craving, of need, insistence. My skin hairs become pert, feel warmed, independent—they have gotten a crush on the sound of a phrase that is so trite when translated; *God is great,* as if saying it makes it true.

زبان خواهر

A chorus: Khareji hasti? Are you a foreigner?

زبان خواهر

I visit the mosque in Nain, the town where my parents' grandparents were born. It is my only visit. How can I help you see the mosque made of bricks in this town I've seen only once, this town from which both my parents descend? If you can't see the color of the bricks, I'll be lying. You'll get to a place you think you know, not the one I know. It's the tide of those already imagined ideas I fight off. For over a decade, I have tried to explain by describing the bricks as butter yellow. Butter yellow: great aunts and uncles in the dust of the courtyard; surely you see them? A mosque, yellow cream, earthy, rooted and rooting me into it. Nain, town of my ancestors. I could take you back two hundred years. A breeze in the courtyard carries the voices of people with my name.

زبان خواهر

None of my relatives would confess to unbelief. Do I shame them when I claim it for myself? They instructed their children how to pray: where to face, how the body changes as it kneels and curves over itself. How soothing to try to get closer to God, or just be outside near the mosque's walls with other people. I eavesdrop and it happens to me, chronically faithless, standing there listening for them: I feel their elbows brush mine, hear the blood moving even under all those clothes.

زبان خواهر

My shadow self: everything I don't say, can't. Or wish I did. But also the self I never had to become, the family's remains buried at the base of a different tree. Thought of by no young mother, missed by no one. The twilight lifetime that lingers in songs other people sing.

زبان خواهر

TEA

: a widely cultivated shrub of the family *Theaceae*

: a reception, snack, or meal at which tea is served

: the drink made by steeping leaves of the tea plant in water heated over a flame. From the 1980s on: definitely not *chai* (chī) the spiced, sweetened Indian drink with added milk.

: in Farsi: *chai* (cha-Ē)

: served in glasses to cup in your palm, though traditional glasses have metal holders for protection.

: where daughters listen to what's important in a life. Where women complain through the sugar cube they're holding in their teeth, and smile when they notice they're crying. Where what's really being drunk is attention.

: space of not-ritual. I learn that there aren't really rules for tea. I like the noisiest women best.

: I perform what I know of hierarchy, of who serves whom, and think *I'll never have daughters who serve me tea,* relieved there's a place for me here. To serve the tea and behave. To look like I know what that means.

: bitter amber drink to wash down sorrow and fear. Tannic tonic, homeroom, safeword. Whisper *chai* when they ask you what you want. It's never greedy.

Syn.
: respite, memory, name among women.

PLEATS

Sister, let's fold time
back on itself, we can
pleat it. We'll push
our needle through the fold,
find silk pants and ruby thread,
pull the Qajar dynasty toward us
with our stitch.
Loop under to anchor, punch
the needle through again and look
for Forugh's poems.
We'll add a flourish and move on,
hips thickening with the ornament
of our history.
We'll go back and visit
the forced unveiling,
when our sisters watched
their futures arrive, like we do,
soak our fabric in the tears
of change—how quickly it absorbs.
We'll bring them code that needs
translation, miniskirts and thigh-highs,
words on the tongues of our men
we need to solve. This pleat
can turn under, part of the
structure of the dress
itself, pinned with a stitch
of our hair, to show it was us
there, whenever the unraveling comes.
When we reach back into
this orphaned future
in which we tuck ourselves, we'll pin
both sides of the rusari at our chins
(to free our hands) and slip things
into our hems: this smart phone,
that Excedrin PM, a degree
in computer science and math.
For what good they do.

SOUNDS LIKE

In the cul-de-sac next street over,
someone sold a Coleman stove for one
dollar at a garage sale, and I came
home with it, saying let's go camping.
I was raised on accented English.
My mother and sister and I were
tree, and when I was a child, that is as green
as my world would get.
The word for *nothing* sounds like
the name of a stoner comedian
named Cheech. I only found out later
he was hilarious. Down the block
a friend had a Persian cat no one
was allowed to touch. Meat loaf, prayers,
old great aunt after school. Before the
phone calls, our cousin's Farsi cheat sheets
fanned out to give us words. We yelled because
they lived across the world. Sometimes they
understood us. We said, how are you.

ARRIVAL

Because I am ready, I find Mohammad.
Or maybe he finds me. Stubbled
and silver haired, he swoops my bags

into the trunk of his cab. Looks me in my eyes.
I form the syllables to where
I am headed, scoot in.

Khareji-am: az California omadam.
He'll hear I'm a foreigner.
I watch my words lumber out

but he smiles into the rearview.
A knot in my brain loosens
so I listen for his next question,

tell him about coming to Iran
to practice Farsi, family in Esfahan,
grandmother's Tehran apartment.

Don't mention I'll be by myself.
How to get him to talk.
What would he say

about his family, the world
he wakes up to, women
who travel alone?

He asks more questions. Am I
married? Do I have children?
I try to respond truthfully. How

happy I am when I'm here, how it feels
to speak. I wonder if there is a Farsi word
for someone like me.

The Only Mistranslation

تنها ترجمه اشتباه

THE ONLY MISTRANSLATION

is belonging. There is no word for it
in any of my tongues. There are
no tongues, so maybe that's my trouble.
How to find a word inside a vacuum.
The din itself is home but home was never
a hearth, and that explains some things.

I belong deep inside my own gut, digesting
seeds rained from my ancestors' dreams,
where compasses keep spinning, where
an avalanche of rare earth
blankets any inkling of sun.

I belong to my own hungry future
never oriented on the map
and never slaked.

A lover once looked down the well of my lungs
and called me nomad. I shook her off
but she was right about a magnet that keeps
moving in the night, stealing off to a different
north.
        Stealing off to a new north
I confound myself, as if I were a butterfly
resisting pins.

ARTIFACTS

In every childhood photo she and I
are dressed like one another.

> By accident, twenty-first century Icelanders
> unearthed a settlement beneath their capital.

Fur-trimmed pantsuits, cherry jumpers,
floral pinafores. This is how I learned to see myself.

> Their atlases were wrong. Where they thought
> their ancestors lived was miles away.

One day the moon consumed my sister's face
and I thought she'd left.

> They'd never had reason to doubt
> where the old turf walls and longhouse stood.

It took me years to see myself. I wondered about the tides
and where they came from, found people who might know.

> An earlier century, previously empty, was now
> populated, full of stories they'd need to learn,

Now a photo in a pile: she is on the floor,
we are wearing the cherries. I have climbed her body.

> add markers to their maps, stand in old places
> with new words for what they know.

I stare into the cavern of my sister's mouth and see her sadness,
the walls of our childhood homes, and the past answers.

> I name what I see.

زبان خواهر

We are in our mother's country. We listen to our mother's tongue. Our language shifts and it shifts us, tectonically.

Biah, I say. You hear it as demand. Chera nemiayi? A complaint. Twin: in our mother's country we cling to each other dizzy with disorientation. Az dellam ta dellet, daughter of my mother. Our tongues divide us. The words haven't changed. But here, when we hear them, we do. I crane my head to find you:

Negah kon.

All the things my sister thinks she doesn't know pull her from me. She doesn't buckle, lets herself be pulled. She is headed into a canyon of silence. She surrenders.

I use all the easy phrases I have, every word I've learned and practiced, each success following another, a line of stones. She gets smaller as she gets farther away, so I turn to retrace my steps. I'm afraid to go too far ahead alone.

زبان خواهر

I board the bus to cross the tarmac and two women, younger than I am, move toward each other to free up a seat for me. They smile at me, talk about their boxes of cookies, say what they are going to do on the island we're headed to in the gulf. I understand whole sentences, can translate their giggles, feel cajoled and embraced, the way I'm meant to.

But no language comes. I had over thirty years of moments before this one, and I recognize the reckless flirtation of phrases, the invitation. Each of those moments have led me here, my tongue split to muteness. I want to giggle back to them, spill laughter over them with words. All I can do is smile, and it is a poverty. They are an island themselves, huddling with their shirini, and I am unmoored and floating away.

زبان خواهر

Noosh-e joon.

I tell the chef of the house how delicious her food is, and she says back, Noosh-e joon. A blessing that goes deep—a giving back of more than just the meal.

Noosh-e joon. I say it now. Sometimes I just say it in my head, because I know the person eating my food doesn't know what it means. But I mean it. It comes without me ever learning it literally. It comes from wanting to keep the gratitude in the open, not shy.

I want to explain:
It has little to do with, *So kind of you to say*. It's close to, *You've tasted my love and given it back to me. I give it back again. I deposit it deep inside you*. I knew all that before I ever had to ask. I even knew it when I pronounced it wrong, said, *moosh*, a word for *cute*, because I could tell how sweet it sounded. I learned it before I learned it. When I say it now, I want to say it raw, I don't want to stop myself, even though I often do. I am intimate. I want to sound like all my aunts who ever said it to me: Hear my love in your ears, swallow it.

زبان خواهر

I have always heard Farsi, though I stopped speaking it when I was very young. There wasn't one moment that my mother suddenly began speaking it to me. Most of my early memories are in the cold, white fake marble entry hallway where I was 3, 4, 5, and my parents are yelling at each other, and my mother is crying. I'm sure I didn't understand the words then, though I understood the meaning: my father, defensive, on his way out; my mother trying to get the scene to end differently.

زبان خواهر

For a summer after my grandmother moved from Iran to LA, we lived with her. After summer school, my sister and I made our way to her house. We'd memorized how to tell her about the bus ride, and we knew we were allowed to throw in English words like *beach* or *shopping*—we knew she knew them. We could tell her when we felt sick, and we knew how to say *school* and *friend* and foods and objects. One day, I got stuck. I felt sure I knew the word for plastic bag and I needed one for a sandwich. I asked her where they were. I stood there, holding my sandwich, waiting, 13 years old. She was confused. "Chi mikhai, azizam? What do you want, sweetie?" "Paa-kat," I repeated, reciting the word for envelope as if all young girls took them to the beach. She started to laugh and moved to the drawers, pulling out a plastic bag, and asked me something like, "Is this what you want?" In Farsi, eyes beaming with affection, she said, "This isn't an envelope, this is a bag." My own eyes lowered. I realized my mistake, and tried to burn the word in my head forever. I wanted to laugh, but I was overwhelmed, annoyed by own muteness. I retreated for the rest of the day. For years, if I'd try to remember the word for bag, I'd think envelope instead.

زبان خواهر

When I speak my Farsi, I see gold flakes floating in the pan. I taste the pomegranate-walnut in the sounds of azizam when my great aunt looks at me from her tiny, scarved head. And the mint dressing she makes is summoned by the words she uses to love me when I am young and nervous at a new school that is near the house where she lives.

When I speak Farsi, I speak imperfectly, hazarding conjugations, connective syllables.

When I speak Farsi I see the thick-toothed smile of my grandmother, sounding out the words in a whisper under her breath. She is rooting for me, in her elegant pants, holding her carefully packed pocketbook, her proud eyes wet.

When I speak Farsi the memories from my childhood are all good ones. I am in a parallel universe of joy and generosity, in my grandmother's Tehran living room, crooked words stretching out in front of me. I am not afraid of who I am—only curious.

When I speak Farsi all the people who love me have their hands on either side of my face. Turn by turn they spend one long moment seeing who they hold, and I see them.

زبان خواهر

It's the women I want to share the most with, who frighten me most because they matter. Is it obvious to them how I want them to say more, how hard I believe if they just kept talking I'd find sentences in my pockets I would pull out and lay around their necks? Everything else is either possible or isn't. The women are who I would have been, though they smile much more and wear more lipstick. They take more chances.

زبان خواهر

WHEN I AM ELEVEN

When I am eleven the six o'clock news says the American hostages are still captive in Iran, going on three hundred days, then four.

When I am eleven my name hasn't stopped being my name. I feel guilty, unpronounceable.

When I am eleven I wonder why my parents came here, why they had their children in a foreign land, hostages of this place, though I understand it is supposed to be my place, and why did they leave us without a good map?

When I am eleven, my sister and I are listening to Casey Kasem's American Top 40 on Sunday mornings, trying to anchor ourselves in pop.

When I am eleven we have school clothes money. I buy a cream-colored shirt which comes with a narrow burgundy tie which I find in the girls' section of a store. Some kids tease me for wearing it the day we take the class picture and I never wear it again.

When I am eleven I don't know about the girlfriend I'll have in college who will want me in a tie so bad she'll buy me one in tomato-red silk.

I think, one day my life will be different, but when I am eleven, I don't understand I can change it. So I stare at my feet when the girls I call my friends throw kickballs at me, and I don't think of names to call back when they say, *eye-ranian freak,* and I don't tell my mother or my sister or anyone else about any of it.

When I am eleven I learn I can get to the ocean on the #8 bus down Carlyle, cross Ocean Ave and PCH, find a spot on the deep and long patch of beach around Lifeguard Station 8, read a book and let the sun cook baby oil into my browning skin.

There, between the pages and the waves, I learn how to walk out and dive under. I let some take me, and I let some knock me down. And I see, sometimes, what it means to let go of who I think I am.

IMMIGRANT

Now that I have learned
the backbend in skirts
and braids, gaze on the horizon
I know is there and I know
knows me, I would not change
anything. These moves keep me
limber enough to see
upside-down. My brain knows
better. Inverted,
I am a beast of burden
carrying myself.
I would not
change anything.
The seafoam green
of the shifting seasons,
the geese I hear
when I can't see, the way
my manicure keeps me
from using my fingers.
It is good exercise, to change
posture, position, remove
the horizon from the equation.
I am oriented to the west
or to the east. It's stasis
that dizzies.
If I try too hard
to stay in the bend, I forget
myself, I take false breaths,
imagine it's easy.
I straighten up to start again.
I breathe deep. Collect
the red blood cells. Draw down.

RECKONING

My cousins know what clings
to them: dust of the border
they crossed, paper boxes
holding the past. They arrive
where I call home. What they choose
is to use a new language.
I thrive by accident.
Divided tongue is my blade
in the wild. I invite the day's light
through all the windows, gaze at pages
where the ink of a country fades.
I don't know whether to trace
the lines or let go.

PASSAGE

In translation, I am a succulent flower
punctuating arid days. I am
a girl without words
listening for a familiar rattle in the seed pods.
I am the book my cousins can't hold
in their hands.
Only in translation, beyond the names
of oceans or latitudes of rice, I belong.
I am in this new place
but haven't noticed yet.

Here I spoon my envy in my cereal,
can't say who it is I'd rather be.
I know the Alborz mountains
but pronounce them without the accent
of absence, the way all my aunts do.
My permits are in order.
I come and go, carrying only their stories
as baggage. I know nothing of exile.
I blink and pass through walls
not meant for me.

DON'T FORGET, THIS IS NOT YOU

I Speak to My Twin Sister

You are not the daughter
about to get swept into the ocean.
I am not that daughter either.

Our grandmothers' grandmothers
will have known.
There are tasks that need doers.

We'll divvy the list.
There has to be a sad girl
and an angry girl.

There has to be one
who likes adults and one
who always scuttles off.

These are our inheritance:
bangles that fixed to our wrists
like the ones we outgrew,

the ones we needed
to be cut from.

A Woman

Here is someone's daughter who wades
into the waves fully garbed
and watches the birds that bobbed there
as they dive into an oncoming surge.
Her foothold falters
and her soaked skirts threaten
to smother her face as the horizon bends
and upends itself in the crash of water
overhead. Over and over, she emerges

to find her footing. She anchors there.
It takes a bit to believe she's standing
again.

All the Women

You are the daughters who appear to be women
though that doesn't make you one.

The coat you are wearing cost a lot of money. Who has that kind of cash?
That woman isn't a woman if she takes gifts from men.

You believe me, don't you?
You, those nights I wonder about loneliness:

Your tattooed lipliner and your laughter
like a line in a poem from childhood.

Or you, your sewing fingers, wanting to stitch
a chador I would wear for you.

You, at your stove with a stew,
the flavor on my gums

of a kitchen I can't fully recall.
My heart's chamber keeps refilling with blood.

There are others like you.
Company when I'm in danger of vanishing

from myself. You are there to love,
so I stay, anchored

to each of you.
                    You leave the surf

to join me for a while, then return.
But mostly you hover in between,

arriving and retreating. As if to say:
no one is ever gone

and no one is only here.

زبان خواهر

I see the woman at the end of the off-ramp in north Tehran. One plastic grocery sack hanging on each wrist and hair tucked in an amber headscarf. She stands on her island of sidewalk, as if expecting someone. Gazes in to each driver, then lets go. Taxi driver says, *she is working*. No one can accuse her of doing anything wrong. She is alone and she is standing and holding her shopping. Her body leans discreetly towards the road. I twist to see her as long as I can.

زبان خواهر

I live alone for a month in Tehran in my grandmother's apartment. I am determined to navigate a capital city of seventeen million, hoping not to stick out, unsure it really matters if I do. When the train pulls into the station I find my way to the women-only Metro car. I'm nervous, sure I'll attract attention. Whatever I do, I will always be the American Iranian who has arranged myself into a long manteau, sleeves pushed down to the wrist for modesty, the top button buttoned over my chest bone and my head wrapped in a pashmina-like hijab—the one thing I wear I think is pretty. I carry something to read, a book that's not in Farsi. I wish it were. I also hold a map, try to keep it hidden. Track the stations as we pass through them. I don't want to miss the one near the Jomeh market, where I'm aimed. I stand for the whole ride. I make way for the older women with their full-length chadors, who drag carts for shopping into our car. Out the window I see young men in short sleeves waiting in a huddle at their stop. I'm trying to reside here, take up the things I've explored before, without depending on family to get me around. I check the map each time the train slows down to stop, and strain to understand the names as they are called on the PA. I feel like I'm holding my breath.

I stop believing I know why I'm here.

زبان خواهر

THE WOMAN IN THE WHITE CHADOR

stands on the flat roof of a house in Masuleh.
Perhaps she left lunch behind on the stove

to edge out onto the layer cake of terraced houses on the hillside,
one row above the other, roofs turning into roads below.

She is not an idea.
Erect, draped, one arm crosses

the bright white of her chest
to hold the swath in place as she looks down.

Leucistic bird: occurrence.
The windows below her are wide open.

The fog rolls up the hill below us,
peers over our shoulders and into all the houses

as if to move us inside.
She could call us to prayer and I would.

She was born where I wasn't.
She is so white she shines

through the muck of others' disbelief.
The day stays foggy.

She is not an idea, and I didn't
put her there. She's not there to jump.

She's there to say she did not jump.

The Word for Heart

کلمه برای دل

THE WORD FOR HEART IS A MEADOW

tie of my tongue   zabaan

                                        love: bring knots

                what comes between them

      us, her wish I could understand   heart's geology

the soul is the dear thing she sees

       sedum, stonecrop,   flower from my name

inventory of my   moons at the bottom of a cup
                                        dokhtare-khoob

           my unripe tongue

      ghaveh   cannot.

                          nemiayid. ma bah hamboodim

           no babies   naboodim

we   tilted
      into shadow   labaan

puzzle solved

laughs when   tongue ties   come loose meadow

ob dod   edgeless meadow

at me, to me, for me she will envelope   I paakat,
        saakat when my voice   sister noise

edge to edge

        so that even now, after

entekhaab mikonam.

                        gold coins   when my muscles are stronger.
                        I ask for sugar. I ask for a ghazal.
                                I memorize everything.

on offer: kalameh, haraf, loghat

        a pail for the words before you're gone. then scatter.

ADVICE FOR A DICTIONARY

Would it help to remind you
there is worse devastation?
On every page words encage other words.
Is there a saw blade sharp enough
to cut through these bars?
Take your pages, reforest our imaginations
with wide boggy meadows and families
that know how to laugh at themselves.
Don't loathe your inherited material.
It's true each day seems finite:
real annihilation is infinite.
The stilt of what I want to say
is also its lilt.
Take the helve of this ax—feel its heft.

JIBRIL

The name of god is in my hands
and you want to hear it.
When my hands
have too much to tell you
I am tongue-tied.
They reach for the dictionary of regret,
they reach for the necklace of longing,
they remember a caress
they haven't yet felt.
Do you feel it? Do you
watch my fingers
when they question the air,
wait for the nameless?
You don't see the stream on the hill
that fed the pond.
The words keep their distance.
I taste them. I wonder how to tell you
what I mean to say, if I am my hands
when you put them to your lips.
The salt on my fingertips
is prayer. What you didn't know
you wanted. Want
is just another word.

It doesn't take long to fall in love with Iran. Between the *fuck this head-scarf, I am so freaking hot* and the loneliness of not being able to sound out letters to make words, or make words into phrases, I watch my father's youngest brother, a man only a few years older than I am, swoon over the great square in Esfahan. He made his fortune starting pizza places and now helps relatives get their footing the same way. He shows me the things he adores about Iran. Says, "Do you know how old these buildings are? Do you see what beautiful architecture was being built here, rival-ing—no, better than—great European cities?" He points to the top of an elaborate domed building and tells me what era the dome was built. He takes me to the garden courtyard of the Abbasi Hotel, on a warm spring night, and we eat a khoresh for dinner, we have tea and sweets. Another afternoon, we pull over on the road near the river where an older woman and her young family roast corn over a giant can stove fire, eating while we stand between the car and the park nearby. He watches with approval as I devour the corn. "Isn't this the BEST," he says, not waiting for my answer. "When I lived in England I tried to make this." And shakes his head.

زبان خواهر

It is a balmy spring weekday and I am walking with a new friend on the grass-lined path next to the Zayandeh River in Esfahan. Hundreds of people are doing the same. In front of us, two men lock arms and clasp their hands as they cross the Sio-se Pol bridge, disappearing into the line of people and thirty-three stone arches. I think of fatwas, I think of the rules this breaks back home. Two men, fond of each other, announcing: *we're friends.*

زبان خواهر

Esfahan is where my father was born, and where I turn 35. I surrender to a compulsion to call him, tell him where I am. I was not alive the last time he went to Iran. He is a shy person, someone who doesn't tell stories of his childhood. For the first time in my life, I can ask him about that time, and he sometimes has something to say. I ask about the scores of stray cats I hear my grandfather cared for, yarns about his tender heart. My father mocks him. Another story he tells just once: he is a teenager, school honors, a prize in his hand, they stroll home together. His father is mute.

Ghormeh sabzi tastes different in Iran, and so does the lamb. I realize that lamb has terroir, like wine. The flavors last long in the mouth, burnished and tender. Eating in Iran is as familiar as my mother's kitchen. So it isn't *that* travel experience. It's this other one: The smell of that working-class obgushteri in Esfahan etches its memory on the meal. Joy from a bowl of soup. Sitting in the courtyard café of Abbasi Hotel on a tart spring evening makes the noodles in the aash-e reshteh a rediscovery of the meals of my childhood, soaked through with lemon and parsley.

زبان خواهر

I had never been in a cherry orchard. When my uncle Saeid learns this, he arranges to drive Monir and me to a friend's, outside the city. We spend the morning moving from tree to tree. I take video on my camera of our stained hands, Monir on a ladder, the lush treetops, the sounds of my lips smacking as I sample the cherries. We are free to be haphazard about the harvest, to pull whole handfuls at once into our baskets and our cardboard boxes, nestle them into the trunk of Saeid's old Peykan, to imagine that the weight of all of them will bring us down closer to the earth as we idle home.

زبان خواهر

I have come to understand that one could get a lifetime crush on Iran. After my first adult trip to Iran, I was embarrassed by this love. I was effusive, ignorant about the privilege of my smooth entry into and out of both my countries. I heard from people who couldn't. Friends eager to see Iran report they'd been told not to try. Relatives were unable to get the paperwork to return to their original home. Or had left the States and, presenting their green cards or provisional cards on return, met the bureaucracy of non-belonging at the US border.

As a welcome, my aunt has stocked the kitchen with the beginnings of delicious meals. She's chopped the vegetables and stewed the meat for the obgusht; she has diced the greens for the ghormeh sabzi.

The meals unfold over our first few days. I'll slurp the soup of the obgusht, and wish I could ask all the questions I don't have the words for. Monir's seasonings conjure sick days when I was a kid. I think of phrases I could use to ask about the upcoming election, but each one feels stiff, translated word by word. I know that more language will help me think differently, and the words will come uninvited, one day. It only feels right to listen, absorb, wait, bite into a tender chunk of lamb, wipe my chin. But it also feels like I'm stifling an opportunity.

I know the food will keep coming. I see the sense in tasting before talking. I remind myself there are other ways to be here, inside language but beside it, too, in order to let my brain change. As if it's sitting in a new chair and needs to learn how to relax back into it and find the right position.

I say to myself: what's different about this meal? How is it changed by eating this dish you've known all your life, here, in Tehran, in your early thirties?

I practice listening.

زبان خواهر

In shops I begin to hear a phrase we never used at home. Ghabel nadareh—which means, literally, it has no worth. I ask about the price of an old wooden box at a bazaar, or a small kilim at the carpet seller's; *it has no worth.* It is a gesture of humility—as if it is not worthy of me, as if I could take it for free. I have to ask again: what is the price? Well, for you . . . The phrase is polite, full of deference for you, the one who might give the seller the honor of buying something; you, the one with power and choice because you possess the money and not the thing. It's a sign to start a relationship. Everyone knows: shopkeepers are the ultimate negotiators, their bargaining is cut throat, there is an ingrained acceptance that the men with the goods are doing you a favor by selling them to you, at whatever price. Even as this contradictory palimpsest is built up, everyone also listens for the ghabel nadareh, the *I am not worthy* chant, the deference with which the changing of money can only take place.

Ghabel nadareh; then the gloves come off. It has no worth, but don't insult me by offering next to nothing. If the bargaining doesn't start off respectfully, neither party will be happy—no matter who "wins." Because it will actually feel like a battle, with a victor, and the unspoken desire is for both people to feel like they had power—that they were able to make choices about money, language, possession, exchange. This can only happen if both sides avoid the temptation to take advantage of the power they begin with.

I say 20 toman, and he says 80. The distance is broachable. We breathe a little easier. Now we can take our time, listen more thoughtfully, to the proposals, feel we've not lost ourselves inside the money that might change hands.

زبان خواهر

I'm apologizing (again) for my scratchy words, my unkempt phrasing. "I just came from California, I—" and I'm interrupted. Dast-e shoma dard nakoneh. May your hands not be hurt by all the effort.

زبان خواهر

I dream my mother leaves me behind at a river crossing. There is a flood that fills streets, makes moats between houses. She makes it to shore. I swim to a rooftop. I'm yelling, Mommy, Mommy and she's saying I know, just let me go to the bathroom first, and I say no, it will be too late. I start screaming help, help, but I know she can't hear me over the rushing water, so I scream louder. I wake up trapped on the top of a roof, without a voice.

زبان خواهر

When I learn to speak Farsi, even the people around me change. Tayebeh, almost an aunt to me, speaks with me in her own tongue for the first time that I can remember, though I've known her since I was a small child. She sounds different in Farsi. We feel different to each other. Her jaw is less nervous, her scope bigger, she is a someone I want to know more.

زبان خواهر

How it feels to be corrected: to not let how it sounded be the right sound.

Or what it feels like to be smiled at with recognition: a face that wants to hear more, wants me to say more. The way Mamanjoon listened. When Farsi words are entrances to a world. When they say, befarmahid.

زبان خواهر

In the bank in Mashhad, I piece together the phrases to explain my hundred dollar bills, I tell the story of my months in Iran and my need for more toman. I am a few months in and I have phrases—chunks of meaning tethered to each other by my smiling, my looking in the eye when I bring out my Farsi. These days I'm less concerned about my own comfort than I am with that of the person who is trying to understand me. Such luxury. The man behind the counter is delighted. He can't stop telling me how good it is that I am there, how important it is that I am coming back to visit my country. No matter how many times I hear it, *my country* startles me. He is a stranger to me, but in these moments, our lack of intimacy isn't relevant—in fact he acts as if I am a niece, like my experience matters. If there weren't other customers, he'd ask me questions. How am I finding things, how long will I stay, where will I go next? Like the cab drivers who ask me about America, but in Farsi, and I realize they want to see who I am. I am a citizen here to look, and it feels so *just* to be looked at back.

زبان خواهر

THE LESSON

What I remember—
my bicycle
my father
training wheels gone
silver of evening
his grip, release
we aim together
I follow him
propel my legs against
an opposing force
but pitch to the ground
he lurches
tips me up
my legs heave
with failure
he moves away
draws me along,
small magnet, moving
up the street
a little farther
he is almost smiling
we are almost
dreaming
the same.

But I can't do it
legs quit, I tip,
crash down
to the lodestone
of earth
and the rough concrete
night also falls
he says, *let's stop*
we walk back to the house
together.

I don't know
it is the last time
he'll be here
in evenings.
Soon I will come again
alone, try to feel him
draw me forward
without knowing
what I'm doing.

I'll pull myself onto
the bike
and tell myself to focus
on a spot ahead
but when I lean
into the pedals I'm only
fighting the bike
and the mass of my own body
nothing keeps me upright
the way I want it to—
my imagination is as unable
to do it as my short,
thin legs.
I'll fall and fall
and then give up.

ROOM 11

My thumb remembers the pieces
of a jigsaw puzzle, waiting to be connected
like we were, my sister and I, when
we were ten years old,
friendless, new in school,
no one home when we went.
Her teacher invited us to stay in the classroom
after the school day was over while she tidied.
She must have seen our faces,
prayer bowls of invitation, eager
to be filled. The two boys were in her class.
The four of us sat at a single table.
We called ourselves the MGPD,
Mentally Gifted Puzzle-Doers.
The name still makes me giddy and proud,
so quickly did it come to mean a club
that would have me, a role written for a self
I recognized and wanted to love.

With a sister who would soon become
more and more opaque
and two boys we barely knew, I owned
this space on a chair in an empty classroom.
I was welcome. My sister had to have me
and for a little while longer we weren't
lost with each other. David and Colin
would turn into blond boys in 1980s
Santa Monica and our circles would barely
make contact again. But that future couldn't change
that little room in my life where we agreed
to complete the edges first, all four corners
and the rest, before assigning ourselves
quadrants or characters or patches
of color, some of us always looking
at the box top, some staring at the table
before us and the scene that was asking

to come together, a hot spot insisting
it be completed ahead of another. A method
for learning to make choices, to take
the next step, live a life.

I shared that room with the three of them,
before the next year, when I'd have to learn
the meanness of other young girls.
I was learning how to keep going
but there's no way I would have known it.
I laughed at Colin's jokes, let my gaze
go soft to see what stood out
in the light, scanned the pile
of cardboard pieces near me,
picked up what was next: the third and fourth
clumps of pumpkin-colored flowers,
a clubfoot looking for its latch.
To puzzle: I develop
a faith in this prayer.
I learn what's next from the pieces
and then I seize them.

NIGHTMARES OR CHI SHOD VAKHTI KHAABIDAM

Stallions of worry break free,
stampede of fierce muscle, knotted jaw.
Yanee chi? The work
of a thousand horses while I sleep?
Donya bozorg-e. Man yek
zanam, vali I am
training for something. It is
as big as the world, as small as
a breath. Bo-ro, bo-ro.
Catch up. It won't wait.

I am in my aunt Monir's kitchen in Mashhad and we are cooking lavoshac, the original Persian version of fruit rollup. We pull the stems off kilos of fresh sour cherries, pull out their pits and drop them into a large pot on the stove. She teaches me the sounds of common talk. I listen with my rough Farsi, often sure I'm mistaken about everything I hear. When her cleaning lady arrives, Monir claims that she is late, tells her she is lazy, mocks her for complaining about something going on in her family. I understand what she says. I am silent, but not because I don't have anything to say. I know Monir feels walled in. The world she thrived in for the first thirty-five years of her life shrank suddenly, after the Islamic Revolution in Iran. I wonder if that meanness to another human was simply her ramming up against those walls. Maybe she would have been mean no matter what had happened to her country. We stir the big kettle of cherries cooking down to what will become a paste, then a dried fruit sheet. The fruit needs to cook slowly, sugars diffusing, flavor deepening.

زبان خواهر

My cousin Bahareh was 16 when I visited her in Esfahan. I was 34. She was born shortly after the Islamic Revolution. While she talks about her country she begins to cry. "I can criticize it, but I love Iran so much and I wish all of us younger people could put it on our shoulders to make it better." After her university entrance exams, she left for several years, went to school in England, then returned to build a career in Iran.

زبان خواهر

Foreigners write Wikipedia entries shrinking the place: list current despots, convince themselves there is little left to know. I—we—Iranians know better. The borders won't hold the people. A bursting could happen.

زبان خواهر

Unveiling

كشف

UNVEILING, IRAN, 1936

She opens her eyes surrounded by flames
   her insides frost-white with possibility
so she wants to split herself open and snow
   on the fire. She smells adoration
in the blaze, glances back from where she came,
   roots her feet by the fire, feels heat
in her tongue. Leans over the hillocks of embers
   as they swell, to see what ardor looks like.
There: as if a mirror. She covers her face
   and cries. She promised to love herself,
but keeps running away.

T W I N

When I am a little girl
I learn to feel the space between
me and my twin sister
as if it is an atomic bond
and we are ions—
the relative connection only shifts
by push and pull. Our peeling apart
is a chemical surprise. Each split
is innocent. She is never mean
by leaving, but she is easily bored
by the games I spend hours with—
jigsaw puzzles and every variation
on the dictionary game I can think of.
I fall blind into the trap of believing
I can keep her here.
I feel unreal when her energy
lessens, when the gleam
of her laughter
casts distracted off our table.
Later, every time my lover's attention
drifts, I reach for my sister's arm
to keep her here, clutch
my reflection in a mirror,
sit it down next to me
and feel the space between us
strangle into stasis.
She turns away and shines her light
on our mirror, refracts back
the deviations. When I am five
I don't know that atomic bonds
are composed of charged particles.
She was the first to learn
how to leave, instructing me
on the solitude of loving.
Now, seeing my own body
next to another makes me
feel alone.

FARNAZ

1.

Our parents argued in a language
we didn't understand. We were born
in Las Vegas or Tehran,

twin cities of fantasy and chance.
My sister and I found our words
in Long Beach, Big Wheels and Barbies,

Bluebird troops and kidnap breakfasts.
A war forced our cousins
to buy false passports, lose their savings.

We ate Chef Boyardee after school,
hot spinach and meatball soup
on the weekends. I yelled into a phone

so my Iranian family could hear me.
I learned I was the silk carpet
my mother didn't own, the casino

payout my father kept chasing.
I didn't know until later
the Persian Leopard was trapped

in the Zagros mountains after
the Iran-Iraq war, in danger
of tripping old mines.

2.

I taught myself who I was
by watching my sister carefully.
I worried when

the day came and I wanted
to say *I'm not her*. First out the womb,
she was named and I wasn't.

Her name is Iranian but sayable
by everyone. My name
would wait. They waited until

they knew they had it right.
Not Sheila, my mother's veto. Farnaz,
a name that made me lonely.

We lived in between Iran
and America, a customs declaration zone.
By the time I was born

my mute parents wondered
how to speak as Americans
as they moved away

from the people who loved them.
How could I know the dark
inside their mouths hurt them, too.

3.

My father studied numbers in the racing forms,
and I bet following my gut.
I influenced dice at the craps table

by spinning three times
in each direction while my father
placed his bets. Even now,

I'll retell stories in my head
one hundred times to end them right.
It's a system.

I came from the racetrack, ignoring
all the horses in the flesh. I sounded out
the names of long shots.

The odds say Blinding Telegram
will win, but I like the music
of Queen the Fox.

I believed that how I got my name would mean something.
I am still finding the names for some things: the youth
my parents brought to parenting, the attention

I didn't know I was waiting for, the word for wanting,
feeling its deep hole. Such naming
I have been slow to do. *I am waiting until I have it right.*

I know that once named there is a road
down which that named thing runs,
and I am not the one who built the road.

My muteness. It is like trying to speak while dreaming. In some dreams I want to yell, which means I know how I feel. I can't say how many times I've wanted to yell in Farsi, but it's not that many. Sometimes I could go far enough in the fantasy that I could understand whole sentences I imagined other people saying. As if I learned this language some deep way when I was very young and my dreamed-up conversations with my aunts and uncles are real.

Is that what is happening when I want to speak Farsi to my uncle Mohammad, a man who has lived in the States for over 50 years? After being in Iran I went to visit and his accented English engaged my Farsi heart—something inside me leapt awake. You won't believe me if I say this surprises me, but it does. I was raised to speak English. I was a suburban southern California kid with a name no one tried to get right. I didn't blame them. The only other Middle Easterner in elementary school was named Shubby Ali. Shubby's family was from Pakistan. He could turn his eyelids inside out.

زبان خواهر

I am leaving Iran after six months. I know I have too much luggage. I'm sent to a special counter to get my bags wrapped, pay extra fees. There is a line but it's not unforgiving and I wait.

He is a small man, like many Iranians, just a couple inches above my head, but he is sitting at his counter on a stool so he is above me. I bring up my bags: a large suitcase, a stuffed duffel, a smaller suitcase, and a santour, strapped and tied into its case. He will weigh them. The man asks me about them. I explain what I have done, how I've fallen in love with the music, how much I'm trying to bring home with me. I tell him the size of the carpets folded up inside, the number of kilims, mention the uncles and aunts who helped me. At first I think I am justifying all the stuff. But then I see his eyes pool, and he says, "You are a daughter of this place and I hope you plan to come back."

He fills out his forms, pressing hard to make the copies, and calculates what I owe, taking my toman from me and shuffling the papers as he stamps them. He hands me the documents and points out where I need to go next, now that my bags are ready. Then he gently gets off of his stool, moves to the side to stand up for me. For emphasis. He says, "It is so good that you came back. What a good thing you did." All I can say is "Thank you," over and over, and then I think I say, "I'm so happy that I came." I walk away from him, looking for the next line, but my heart is beating so fast my face heats up, and the airport around me is a blur.

زبان خواهر

I try for several months to write a poem. Instead, I write an op-ed that I read to audiences called, "You Should Go to Iran." I want to introduce Americans to the young women I meet who say they are comfortable with headscarves, to the strangers who invite Americans into their homes and feed them sweets and tea. This takes place in the months immediately following 9/11. I feel funneled to the center of a much bigger storm than an individual could ever quell. It feels like I'm saying the same thing over and over—Don't ruin my country—except that I stumble on the word *my*.

I am trying to explain what it feels like to have not come from a place and to have come from the very same place.

زبان خواهر

I learn to read the Farsi alphabet in the backseat of a Volkswagen bug with my sister and two girl cousins, their parents and my mother. We are driving from Tehran to the Caspian Sea and I am not yet seven years old. I will keep this book my whole life. I know sounds and words already, but have never looked at them on the page. On each page, large letters: we see بابا baba and the picture of the father, we learn beh. My aunt points to a sound, and I say it. آب Ob. Water. Now I see it on the page. Grasping the way the letters fit together to make the words doesn't seem out of reach. I take a pencil, trace the dotted lines on a page, do it over and over in each of the spaces left to do it, feel myself learning. My sister does it too. Neither of us is nervous. Other people are watching, but right now they are encouraging, and I'm not afraid to mess anything up. They don't seem to mind helping us learn letters during this hot ride north. Years later my aunt can still recall the trip. "Do you remember that trip to the sea? How many of us were all in that car!" I say, "I learned to read the aleph-beh on that trip." "Yes! You two were working so well on your letters. I remember the books." I can see she wants to pinch my cheek, or muss my hair. But I'm an adult now, and she just smiles wide, and I can see her remembering the kid versions of us, her daughters and nieces, and then she remembers to see me now, beautiful and grown up, still practicing my reading.

زبان خواهر

There were famous singers of famous songs that the young martyrs of the war with Iraq listened to before running out to be killed. They had these voices in their head as they ran.

زبان خواهر

Language is geological: a process of accumulation and accretion, accompanied by landslides. I have to do my best to keep adding to the pile, while not giving up when a storm comes along to upturn it. I say this to myself a thousand times.

زبان خواهر

If someone says, you're beautiful, the phrase in response is, your eyes just see so beautifully.

زبان خواهر

My shadow self. Everything I don't say, can't. Or wish I did. But also the self I never had to become, the family's remains. The twilight lifetime that lingers in songs other people sing.

I was the kind of kid who didn't question the systems, a girl who kept her mouth shut. I welcomed the chance to be obedient. There was an order to that. A promise that it might matter in my own personal future, if I was or I wasn't. Like many young women, when I got to college, I learned that my obedience hadn't mattered much at all.

Outside the apartment door in Esfahan, on the street, two twentysomething women lean in close to each other, smiling, as they stroll by. One says something emphatically, leans closer and puts her hand on her friend's arm near the shoulder. "Do you know what I mean?" she says as she slaps her friend on the arm, then leaves her hand there as they continue. They are lost with each other to the circumstances of the street: they don't see me, they could be anywhere. They're not: their headscarves are tied, their makeup just moderate enough, but their hearts are spilling out onto all of them, and even this foreigner can see it. I am not that woman, though I've long wanted to be. Long watched women this effusive, this gushing about whatever it is they feel, long known how close I am to the emotion, how far from the physical gestures of it. I remember my aunt Monir's loud laugh when I was young and how it scared me. How I was afraid other things would disappear inside that mouth, that her joy could consume people around her, or me, on a summer visit from another land—I might be swallowed by the size of her laughter.

زبان خواهر

SISTER
Mehrabad Airport, Tehran

Outside the terminal doors
we are a crushing predawn crowd,
we swarm out between the glass exits
and the taxi stands:
on one side, my grandmother,
the other, my mother.
My first visit
since my grandfather's death.
The sister disembarks,
trails us by meters,
is round, middle-aged,
draped in black veils and skirts.
She begins to scream in anguish
sags with the folds of cloth, downward,
drops to her knees
arcs her arms upward,
over her head
then down, like two axes, down
while she cries,
as if to pray and thresh the ground
in punishment,
pray and punish
pray and punish.

She is wailing:
My brother—
my brother,
the only one I had.
I only had one brother
my brother
he was the only one I had.
Strangers, a dozen deep,
surround her, drawn by the keening
of her loss.
Her pitch rises as her body falls

sideways, she leans there.
The only one I had.
A ring of women,
now wailing,
reach her.
The sky above us swells
with their sounds.

We hover near the sister,
my grandmother's face opens wide
cheeks flush, eyes pooling,
my mother's face an answer
lips trembling, parted.
And my aunt's, my sister's, my heart
all flail open
toward this crooning
while my grandfather's memory takes shape
between us, sprung loose
as if by incantation:
He was the only one I had.

LIMINAL

To know a place as if I could dig
a hole in the yard and reach it.

What I don't know I know:
Pakistan to me

before it bordered Iran to the east:
the other Middle Eastern kid.

The calcite in which I keep
a place encircled by seven countries.

How does a line
make the fabric shimmer more?

To love a place and learn it—
Who pilloried? Who praised?

Fossil of my father's shame,
family gravestones, all the ways

to pronounce the word for breath.
Loyalty keeps watch and

it doesn't know what risk means.
I can't be contained.

I want to know where
my Jewish husband belongs.

I am divided by my attachments,
limestone walls at odds, bounding

my world.

SWORD-SHAPED HEART

In the *Birder's Dictionary* I read about a bone
near the bird's heart, called xiphoid,

meaning sword shaped. My fingers reach for my ribs.
If my father's anger were shaped like his swimming pool

instead of a sword, he could sink down
under the surface and listen.

I could return my sword-shaped heart
and pick out something else.

If my husband's pain were cup shaped,
he could add milk, then drink.

I'd cut out my tongue
and grow a more tender one.

If the martyr's vision landed on his mother's oleander,
he could soak up the rich scarlet of its flowers.

His mother could join him. They could stare and exclaim.
I could dream up a new language

to speak to martyrs.
If all the fathers could find themselves

on the maps they're born with, they could free their eyes
to look that way.

I would wait on the road, ready to paint a ruby X
to mark their spot.

AFTER THE WARS

He wants her to teach him
where gentleness comes from.

How her hands fashion this life
when they were born of electric fences

and fused knots.
He thinks, I am afraid

I am only the person I was when I was born.
She sees this sentence in his eyes.

Kisses his eyelids when he sleeps.
He dreams of his own hands

as a boy, once hairless and soft,
his left holding his own right.

He dreams of jump ropes
and toy cars. In sleep, he smiles.

She considers his invitation
to teach him to be soft,

how to help with the laundry,
love loudly. They won't

have children. This will be plenty.

HERETIC

When you sang your body invented us
    an alphabet. No one heard it
      but me.

The earth in your eyes
    is the ink in your words.
      Each look writes another line.

Everything I need to know grows wings
    and lands on my skin.
      A thousand tiny plovers

cover the skies, and shine
    like moonlight on us both,
      turning us into your verses.

Last night each dot and curve of the letters of our alphabet
    came to rest on my body while I slept,
      entwined around my hips,

pulled their fingers through my hair.
    I breathed them in. Became the song
      you sang me.

You spell the morning prayer
    uttered by my lips.
      Syntax of attention

at the back of your throat. Each rise in note
    is your hand on my ribs.
      You hold me and no one can see.

Our unholy wholeness hides.
    Your name in the nearness. Says listen.
      Sentences of rebellion

in the starless night.

WHAT KIND OF WOMAN

Before we came she'd combed her hair,
put on the beaded earrings
my mother made her.

She'd shrunk.
The earrings were small stacks
of seven beads: three crystals

between four gold disks.
They shone. Enough
to show she was trying.

When she died
I asked for that pair.
I'm the granddaughter

who moved away.
The kind of woman who forgets
to take them off to sleep.

I say out loud: I'll wear them
until I lose one.
Scan a mirror for a hint of her.

One goes missing
in just a week.
A friend finds it,

asks if the earring is mine.
I think, No—.
Yes—. For a little longer.

WHEN I KNEEL, I DON'T THINK OF A GOD

I think of you, and you, and also you,
so long gone, now, I'm not telling your stories,
I don't invoke you to explain laughter.
I have other beloveds nearby
I watch to learn how to live,
close to the tip of my tongue, like you were.
You do not linger out loud.
You are not in my mouth.

But it's not what you think. Now—
like the idiom I'd only heard, but never
bit into, couldn't have swallowed—
you are in my liver. No, you are my liver.
That's what I can say, when I pray:
jigar-e-man, my liver,
teach me what to do now.

زبان خواهر

Late April. I'm picking up the phone for the first time to call someone in Farsi.

I'm making my first friend, here. We go out for Turkish coffee and talk about her life. She tells me it's her fate to not be married. I listen, repeat the word for fate in my head when she says it, think about whether I agree. In the grounds at the end of the coffee, I tell her I see an ear in her cup, knowing this is what happens when women are done with their coffees—they read them. She says, "Oh, listen to what your mother tells you." I say, "No, listen to what your heart says," piecing together the nouns and the possessive forms correctly, "I can hear." She stares hard into the cup, and I can see she is smiling under her hard face. I am trying to share who I am and she is paying attention.

زبان خواهر

When I'm alone, wherever I am, I am often talking to myself out loud. I figured out that as an adult, it's how I know I'm listening. I mean in English. One morning in the middle of a month in Iran I commend myself about my Farsi, and I say it in Farsi. And then I say, in English: see, it's goofball Farsi, but it's yours, and that's how it's going to have to be. I am looking in the mirror in my grandmother's apartment in Tehran. I have the place to myself. In a couple of years, she will sell it to one of my cousins. She will never be back here.

Looking at myself putting on my headscarf, getting ready to go outside, get a taxi, visit some relatives, I recognize myself. And I recognize the voice I'm using, but it's different. I have things to say in Farsi, things that won't translate. Things I can't say any other way.

زبان خواهر

ACKNOWLEDGMENTS

Thank you to the editors at these publications where versions of poems from this collection have appeared:

Catamaran Literary Reader, Community of Writers Review, Crab Orchard Review, Essential Voices: Poetry of Iran and Its Diaspora, Grist, Halal If You Hear Me, Jung Journal: Culture and Psyche, Let Me Tell You Where I've Been, My Shadow Is My Skin, phren-Z, Poets.org, The Shore, The Signal House Edition, Tahoma Literary Review, and *Tupelo Quarterly.*

Thanks to editors Jeremy Reed, Leila Emery, and Katherine Whitney, who published versions of the lyric essay that is this book's spine. Persis Karim, who connected me to a community of writers in the Iranian Diaspora. Cassandra Cleghorn, who I met by pure luck, who invited me to write across a border I had long imagined existed between genres, to make the work I needed.

So much love and appreciation for my poetry sisters, mis poetas, who I found after a time of loss: Lisa Allen Ortiz, Frances Hatfield, Ingrid LaRiviere, and Danusha Laméris. They helped me notice *Sister Tongue* as it came to be now; they are the teachers I always wanted. More generous poets have all closely read poems in this book: Charles Atkinson, Tilly Shaw, Terri Drake, Dion Farquhar, Maggie Paul, Roxi Power, David Swanger, Robert Sward, Carmen Fought, Seth Hagen, Harry Griswold, Terry Spohn, Nicelle Davis, and Jessica Koong. Erica Gillingham and Ingrid LaRiviere gave so much of their time, their vital feedback, and their friendship to this work.

I am indebted to each family member who tethers me to real places and to those who have housed me in those places. Many of them have listened to my goofball Farsi, but I need to name Mamanjoon and Sahar Fatemi, both of whose joy for my tentative tongue made all the difference. Thank you to my mother, Fereshteh Fatemi, for giving me Farsi grammar advice even when my spelling makes her cringe. To Matt, Sarah, and Jason Skenazy, with whom I have bonded in ways that go beyond received concepts of family-tude. And thanks are not enough to my sisters Shahla Fatemi and Tara Walker who are with me everywhere.

I am grateful to poet friends for their belief in my work spanning many years: Melissa Fondakowski, Roz Spafford, Roxi Power, and David Sullivan. To Marge Frantz and Parviz Azad, who always wanted me to keep writing. To Brenda Shaughnessy and T Kira Madden for their generosity and their particular rigor. To my mother and my aunts Farideh Azad and Hamideh Fatemi, who modeled passion for their art.

To the residency spaces whose gifts of time helped make this book: PLAYA, Djerassi, Marble House Project, Vermont Studio Center, and I-Park Foundation. To David Hassler and everyone at the extraordinary Wick Poetry Center, to the entire staff at Kent State University Press, and to Tracy K. Smith for choosing this book.

I don't know how to thank the Iranian teen girls who let me ask them questions over the years and the twenty- and thirty- and fortysomething women I was almost too afraid to talk to. I try to honor them.

I am fortunate to have people in my life who might not be big poetry readers but who have still come to a reading, bought publications, or described to me how my work reached them. You know who you are, and I do too. I am also lucky to have Paul, the life we've shaped that allows all of this in it, and the treasured way you love me.

NOTES

"Heretic" was written in conversation with photographs by Shirin Neshat. "Pleats" was inspired by photographer Shadi Ghadirian's series *Qajar*. "Don't Forget, This Is Not You" borrows its title from a photograph by Newsha Tavakolian. The catalog from the exhibition *She Who Tells a Story: Women Photographers from Iran and the Arab World* was given to me by my friend Diana Rothman; *Sister Tongue* came to life inside the world of that show.

"Tea" is for Elham Sheikh, who helped me see tea (and family) anew when she made space for me in her home in Esfahan.